TIMELINE HISTORY

WORK

From Plows to Robots

Elizabeth Raum

Heinemann Library
Chicago, Illinois

www.heinemannraintree.com
Visit our website to find out more information about Heinemann-Raintree books.

To order:
☎ Phone 888-454-2279
🖳 Visit www.heinemannraintree.com to browse our catalog and order online.

© 2011 Heinemann Library
an imprint of Capstone Global Library, LLC
Chicago, Illinois

Edited by Louise Galpine and Diyan Leake
Designed by Richard Parker
Original illustrations © Capstone Global Library Ltd 2011
Illustrated by Jeff Edwards
Picture research by Hannah Taylor

Originated by Capstone Global Library Ltd
Printed and bound in China by CTPS

14 13 12 11 10
10 9 8 7 6 5 4 3 2 1

Library of Congress Cataloging-in-Publication Data
Raum, Elizabeth.
 Work : from plows to robots / Elizabeth Raum.
 p. cm. -- (Timeline history)
 Includes bibliographical references and index.
 ISBN 978-1-4329-3806-2 (hbk.) -- ISBN 978-1-4329-3814-7 (pb) 1. Labor--History--Juvenile literature. 2. Occupations--History--Juvenile literature. I. Title.
 HD4841.R38 2011
 331--dc22
                          2009049021

Acknowledgments
The author and publisher are grateful to the following for permission to reproduce copyright material: Alamy Images p. 11 (© Ace Stock Limited); Corbis pp. 4 top (Sygma/Frédéric Soltan), 4 bottom (Peter M. Fisher), 6 top (Bettmann), 15 top (The Gallery Collection), 15 bottom (Finbarr O'Reilly), 19 top (John H. Tarbell), 20 top (Underwood & Underwood), 22 (John Springer Collection), 23 bottom (Bettmann), 24 (Bettmann), 25 top (Ryan Pyle), 26 (epa/Waltraud Grubitzsch), 27 bottom (Digital Art); Getty Images pp. 6 bottom (Robert Harding/David C. Poole), 9 (The Bridgeman Art Library), 10 top (Time Life Pictures/Mansell), 12 (Panoramic Images), 13 bottom (Robert Harding/Gavin Hellier), 17 top (Hulton Archive), 18 (Hulton Archive), 19 bottom (Time Life Pictures/Mansell), 20 bottom (Hulton Archive), 23 top (Hulton Archive); Mary Evans Picture Library p. 16; NASA p. 27 top; Photolibrary pp. 7 (The Print Collector), 13 top (North Wind Pictures), 14 (North Wind Pictures), 17 bottom (North Wind Pictures), 21 (The Print Collector); Rex Features p. 25 bottom (Sipa Press); The Art Archive p. 10 bottom (Dagli Orti); The Bridgeman Art Library p. 8 top (Giraudon/National Museum, Damascus, Syria).

Cover photograph of robotic arms in a car factory reproduced with permission of Corbis (Gideon Mendel).

Every effort has been made to contact copyright holders of material reproduced in this book. Any omissions will be rectified in subsequent printings if notice is given to the publisher.

Contents

Historical time is divided into two major periods. BCE is short for "Before the Common Era"—that is, the time before the Christian religion began. This is the time up to the year 1 BCE. CE is short for "Common Era." This means the time from the year 1 BCE to the present. For example, when a date is given as 1000 CE, it is 1,000 years after the year 1 BCE. The abbreviation *c.* stands for *circa*, which is Latin for "around."

Any words appearing in the text in bold, **like this**, are explained in the glossary.

Thinking About Work

One of the most common questions that adults ask children is "What do you want to be when you grow up?" What they mean, of course, is "What kind of work do you want to do?" There are lots of choices. Some jobs—farming, fishing, and cooking—are thousands of years old and continue today.

These fishermen in India are doing work that people have done for thousands of years.

Other jobs, like being a television actor or computer **technician**, are much newer. These jobs did not exist before the invention of television and computers. As the world changes, so do our jobs.

This book takes a look at how work has changed, from when people first lived on Earth through the present. It cannot include all types of jobs, of course, but it provides an introduction to the history of work, from plows to robots.

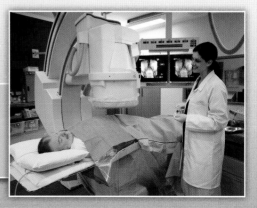

The invention of medical machinery has meant there are many new kinds of jobs in the modern world.

Timelines

The information in this book is on a timeline. A timeline shows you events from history in the order they happened. The big timeline in the middle of each page gives you details of a certain time in history (see below).

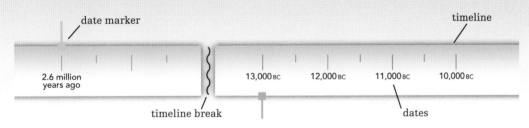

Some dates are not exact because early people did not keep written records. Other dates cover decades or centuries because they show what happened over a general period of time rather than on a precise date. The smaller timeline at the bottom of each page shows you how the page you are reading fits into history as a whole. You will read about work from all around the world. Each entry on the main timeline is in a different color. This color shows you which continent the information is about. The map below shows you how this color coding works. Pale green indicates events that took place in more than one continent or worldwide.

Working to Eat

Early people hunted or gathered everything they ate. They began farming about 7,000 years ago. People grew **grains** and peas in the **Middle East**, rice in China, and corn in the Americas.

2.6 million years ago   TOOLMAKER

The very earliest people probably used rocks as tools. In Ethiopia, **archaeologists** discovered scraping and cutting tools that are about 2.6 million years old. These tools were made by hand. Over time, tools improved. Ancient toolmakers made axes, spears, and tools that could be used to plant seeds or dig for roots.

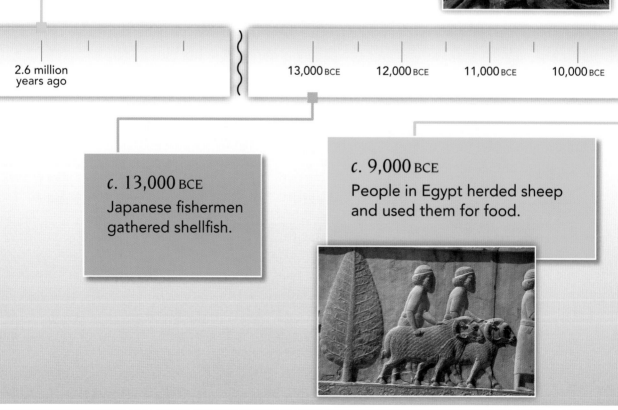

| 2.6 million years ago | 13,000 BCE | 12,000 BCE | 11,000 BCE | 10,000 BCE |

c. 13,000 BCE
Japanese fishermen gathered shellfish.

c. 9,000 BCE
People in Egypt herded sheep and used them for food.

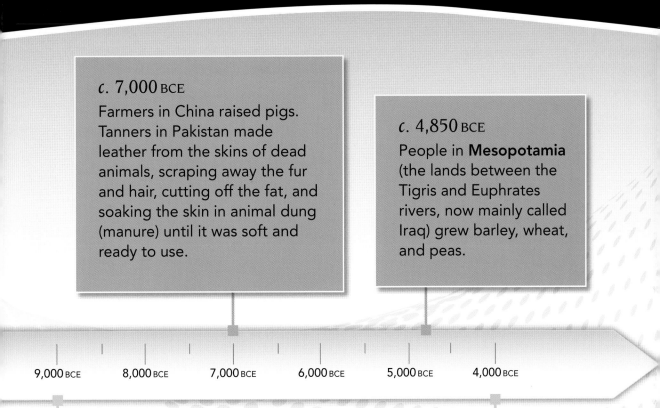

c. 7,000 BCE

Farmers in China raised pigs. Tanners in Pakistan made leather from the skins of dead animals, scraping away the fur and hair, cutting off the fat, and soaking the skin in animal dung (manure) until it was soft and ready to use.

c. 4,850 BCE

People in **Mesopotamia** (the lands between the Tigris and Euphrates rivers, now mainly called Iraq) grew barley, wheat, and peas.

9,000 BCE   8,000 BCE   7,000 BCE   6,000 BCE   5,000 BCE   4,000 BCE

c. 4,000 BCE

Farmworkers in Egypt used plows to make farming easier. Today, farmers depend on tractors and combine harvesters.

Building Towns and Cities

As villages and cities grew, kings, **pharaohs**, and emperors took charge. These leaders chose people they trusted to be **civil servants**. Civil servants supervised day-to-day activities, such as collecting taxes, keeping order, and building pyramids and palaces.

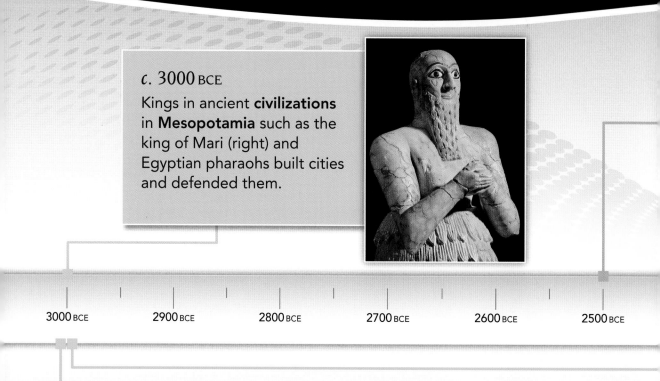

c. 3000 BCE

Kings in ancient **civilizations** in **Mesopotamia** such as the king of Mari (right) and Egyptian pharaohs built cities and defended them.

3000 BCE	2900 BCE	2800 BCE	2700 BCE	2600 BCE	2500 BCE

c. 3000 BCE SLAVES

No one knows exactly when or how slavery began. A **slave** is a person who is the property of another. The Egyptians used slaves to build the great pyramids. So did the Sumerians, who lived in Mesopotamia. Slaves did the heavy work, such as cutting blocks of stone and hauling heavy loads.

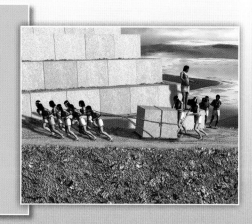

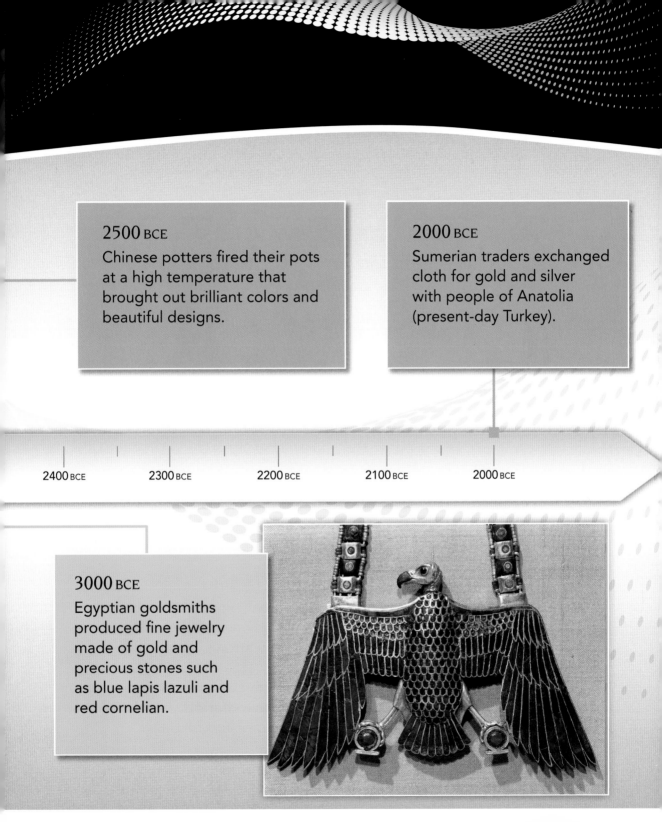

2500 BCE
Chinese potters fired their pots at a high temperature that brought out brilliant colors and beautiful designs.

2000 BCE
Sumerian traders exchanged cloth for gold and silver with people of Anatolia (present-day Turkey).

2400 BCE | 2300 BCE | 2200 BCE | 2100 BCE | 2000 BCE

3000 BCE
Egyptian goldsmiths produced fine jewelry made of gold and precious stones such as blue lapis lazuli and red cornelian.

Competing for Power

During ancient times, soldiers helped rulers gain power through warfare. The Hittites (in present-day Turkey) battled Assyrian and Egyptian armies during the 1200s BCE. In the 800s BCE, Greek city-states fought for power. Lawmakers, **philosophers**, and teachers worked to bring order to the world.

Mid-1700s BCE
Hammurabi, king of Babylon (on his throne, right), wrote laws to settle disputes and bring order. Laws led to jobs for lawyers, judges, and record keepers.

1600–1000 BCE
During China's Shang **dynasty**, fortune-tellers wrote questions on animal bones and heated them. They studied the cracks to predict the future.

1800 BCE 1700 BCE 1600 BCE 1500 BCE 1400 BCE 1300 BCE 1200 BCE 1100 BCE

1274 BCE
Egyptian and Hittite soldiers used bows and arrows, spears, knives, and clubs. High-ranking warriors drove **chariots** or rode horses into battle.

776 BCE   THE FIRST OLYMPICS

The first Olympic games were held in Greece. Athletes raced 192 meters (630 feet) to see who was fastest, as shown on this vase. Jumping, discus throwing, and wrestling became Olympic sports at later games.

| 1000 BCE | 900 BCE | 800 BCE | 700 BCE | 600 BCE | 500 BCE | 400 BCE |

700s BCE

Greek shipbuilders designed boats that used sails on windy days and oars on calm days. Sailors were able to surprise their enemies by rowing quietly close to their camps.

551–479 BCE

Confucius, a Chinese teacher and philosopher, taught that rulers must make honorable decisions. He lived during China's North-South dynasties.

Building for the Future

Buildings and roads that were created 2,000 years ago still exist today. The music, literature, and poetry of ancient people have also survived into modern times.

400–300 BCE

The first mail carriers rode horses to deliver messages in the region that is now part of Turkey. They changed horses at stations along the route.

400–300 BCE

In ancient India, actors, dancers, and poets provided entertainment.

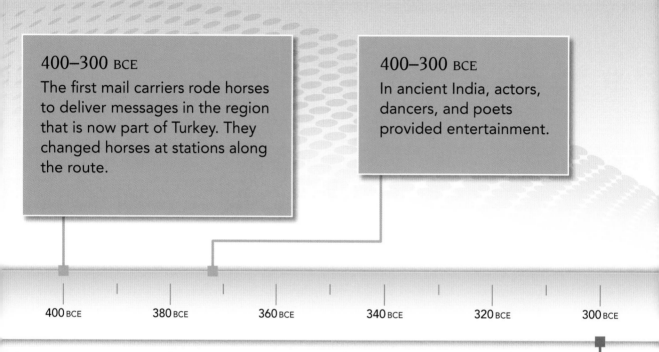

400 BCE	380 BCE	360 BCE	340 BCE	320 BCE	300 BCE

300–200 BCE   CONSTRUCTION WORK

Thousands of construction workers built temples, dug roads, and created waterways in ancient Rome. Most public buildings were made of mud and clay bricks, with large marble slabs cemented onto the fronts. They were held together with concrete, which was made of dust from volcanoes, **lime**, and water. To make roads, workers dug foundations 1.2 to 1.5 meters (4 to 5 feet) deep. They used layers of rock to fill the foundations and create a flat road surface.

200 BCE

In Alexandria, Egypt, works by great writers were gathered to create one of the world's first and largest libraries. The books were in the form of rolled scrolls of papyrus, a type of paper made from a plant that grew nearby.

| 280 BCE | 2600 BCE | 240 BCE | 220 BCE | 200 BCE |

200 BCE

In Peru, musicians played wind instruments called pan pipes. Pan pipes were made from hollow cane, bone, and clay. People still play pan pipes today.

Serving Royalty

Rulers needed thousands of people—including farmers, dye-makers, and tax collectors—to keep their empires running. Many jobs were performed by **slaves**.

400 BCE

In Mexico, dye-makers used cochineal insects to make bright red dye for royal cloaks. Cochineal dye is still used today.

700s CE

In Japan, tax collectors gathered cloth and other products for the emperor's government.

400 CE

700 CE 800 CE 900 CE 1000 CE 1100 CE 1200 CE

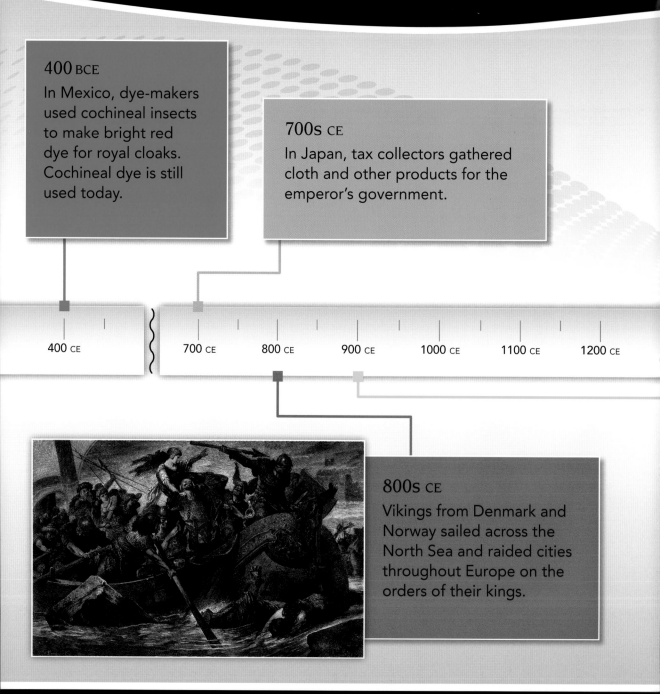

800s CE

Vikings from Denmark and Norway sailed across the North Sea and raided cities throughout Europe on the orders of their kings.

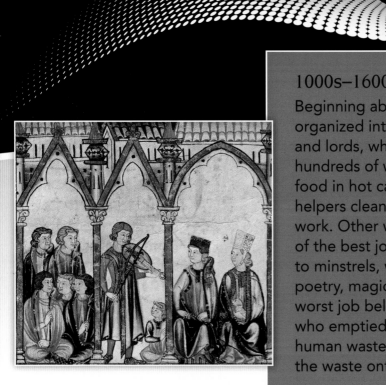

1000s–1600s CE CASTLE JOBS

Beginning about 1000 CE, Europe was organized into small kingdoms. Kings and lords, who lived in castles, employed hundreds of workers. Cooks prepared food in hot castle kitchens, and kitchen helpers cleaned up. Peasants did the farm work. Other workers herded the pigs. One of the best jobs at the castle belonged to minstrels, who entertained with music, poetry, magic, and juggling. Perhaps the worst job belonged to the gong farmer, who emptied the latrine, the pit where human waste was dumped, and spread the waste onto farm fields.

1300 CE   1400 CE   1500 CE   1600 CE   1700 CE

900s CE

Slaves mined salt in north Africa. Traders carried the salt by camel **caravans** to west and central Africa. People paid for the salt in gold.

Expanding Our Knowledge

From the 1200s to the 1500s, people learned about unknown worlds—both on Earth and in outer space. New ways of printing books, the journeys of explorers, and advances in **astronomy** provided new jobs, as well as exciting adventures.

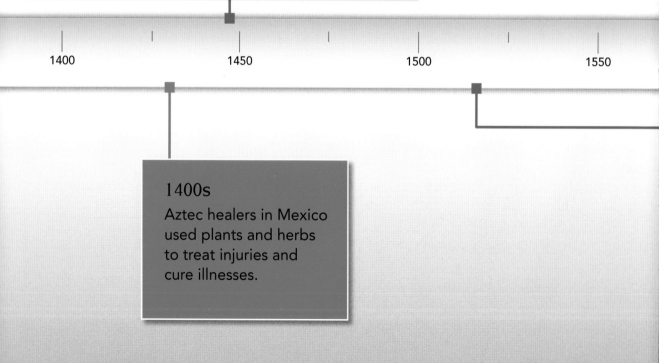

c. 1448 PRINTERS AND PUBLISHERS

Johannes Gutenberg set up the first printing press, in Mainz, Germany. In earlier times, scribes copied books by hand. The printing press was faster and cheaper. It allowed writers, illustrators, and publishers to create new books. As the number of books increased, so did the number of people who learned to read.

1400   1450   1500   1550

1400s

Aztec healers in Mexico used plants and herbs to treat injuries and cure illnesses.

2.6 million �
years ago

1400s–1600s

In Italy, astronomers such as Galileo and Copernicus developed new ideas about the universe by studying the stars.

Mid-1400s–1600s

Portuguese **slave** traders took 175,000 Africans to Europe and the Americas. Most ended up in Brazil, the Caribbean, and Spanish **colonies**, where they were forced to work as miners and farmers.

| 1600 | 1650 | 1700 |

1400s–1500s

In the 1400s, explorers from Spain and Portugal reached the Americas, India, and Japan. In the 1500s, they explored parts of Africa, Australia, and the Arctic. Magellan's crew was the first to sail around the world.

Changing the Way We Work

The **Industrial Revolution** began in England around 1750. Products once made at home, such as cloth, were now made by machines. Factory jobs brought workers to the city.

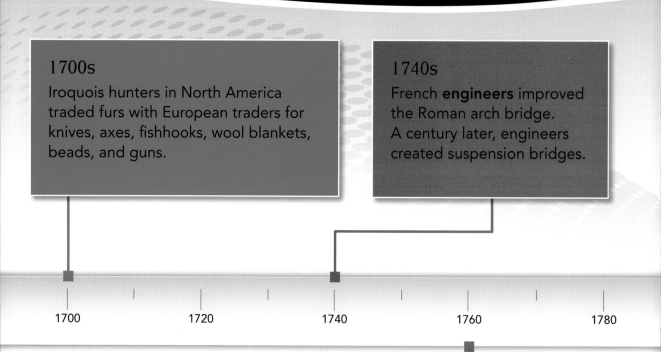

1700s

Iroquois hunters in North America traded furs with European traders for knives, axes, fishhooks, wool blankets, beads, and guns.

1740s

French **engineers** improved the Roman arch bridge. A century later, engineers created suspension bridges.

1700   1720   1740   1760   1780

1760s

Factory workers in England spent up to 12 hours a day doing boring jobs in poorly lit factories. Accidents were common, but workers did not complain. They feared losing their jobs.

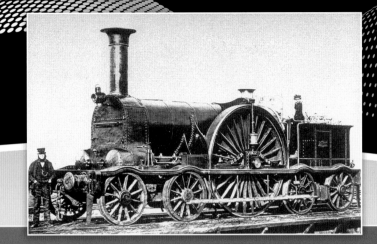

1830s RAILROAD WORKERS

The steam engine made train service possible, first in Great Britain, and then across the world. As train service grew, so did jobs connected to the railroads. Workers dug foundations and laid track. They tunneled through mountains, working long days for little pay. The best jobs belonged to engineers who drove the trains, firemen who kept them running, and conductors who scheduled them.

| 1800 | 1820 | 1840 | 1860 | 1880 |

1860

The first camel drivers from central Asia arrived in Melbourne, Australia, to provide transportation across the continent's enormous deserts.

1865

When the Civil War ended in the United States, freed **slaves** found work on farms or as maids, cooks, or nannies. Others traveled to northern cities for factory work.

Making New Connections

New inventions such as the telephone and the typewriter created new jobs. Many of these jobs paid little and were filled by young women. Workers campaigned for better rights and working conditions.

1830 MAKING THE WORLD ELECTRIC

Inventors found ways to use electricity to light homes and run appliances. By the 1880s, electricians worked to bring electricity into homes in the United States and Europe (and later in other areas). They installed electric poles and wires all across the world. Today, electricians install new wiring and lineworkers fix and replace poles and wires.

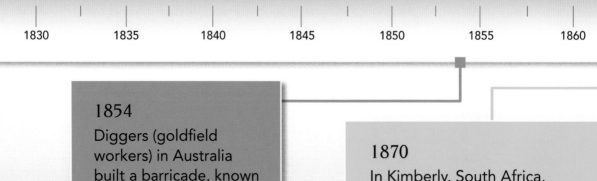

```
1830      1835      1840      1845      1850      1855      1860
```

1854

Diggers (goldfield workers) in Australia built a barricade, known as the Eureka Stockade, to protest against an unfair government tax. The rebellion was put down violently, but the diggers eventually won their case.

1870

In Kimberly, South Africa, miners dug 1,097 meters (3,520 feet) into the earth to find diamonds. Diamond cutters and diamond merchants prepared the diamonds for sale.

1874

With the invention of the typewriter in the United States, secretaries could prepare reports and letters quickly. Today, most office workers use computers.

1878

Switchboard operators in the United States connected one caller to another. Now calls go through an automatic switchboard.

1870   1875   1880   1885   1890   1890

1890s

In Germany, the invention of X-ray machines made it possible for radiologists to see inside the human body.

Amusing Ourselves

People found new ways to amuse themselves after long hours at work. There were movies, radio programs, and cartoons for entertainment. Very rich people traveled throughout the world.

1894 MOVING PICTURES

In the United States, the first movie, *Fred Ott's Sneeze*, showed an actor sneezing. Other early movies showed everyday life—trains, firefighters at work, and street scenes. Later movies told stories. Cameramen, directors, **producers**, and actors worked making movies (right). The first movies were silent. Piano players or organists played during the movie. Today, thousands of people work in the movie industry.

1890   1895   1900   1905

1900s

In the United States, Wilbur and Orville Wright invented the first airplane. Soon people found jobs building planes. Pilots, flight attendants, ticket sellers, baggage handlers, and travel agents worked with airlines.

1908

In France, cartoonists drew the first animations by hand. Today, most animators use computers.

1909

Soon after he left office, U.S. president Theodore Roosevelt traveled to Uganda and Kenya on a year-long safari. Five hundred porters (people who carry supplies), guards, cooks, and servants went along. So did naturalists—experts in plants and animals. Today, safari companies employ hundreds of workers in Africa.

1910   1915   1920

1920s

Radio provided news from around the world. This radio announcer reported on the Olympic Games from Paris, France.

Leaving This World Behind

The invention of television and computers created many new jobs. As the **space program** began, thousands of scientists and **engineers** helped us to reach outer space.

1940–present

Television writers, directors, and actors develop programs. Camera operators and sound **technicians** keep everything working.

1950

Computers still employ lots of people as **programmers**, salespeople, teachers, technicians, and designers. This book was designed and written on a computer.

1940　　　1950　　　1960　　　1970

1961

The Russian pilot Yuri Gagarin was the first person in space. He flew in the cabin of a spacecraft like the one shown and was called a cosmonaut. Americans who go into space are called astronauts.

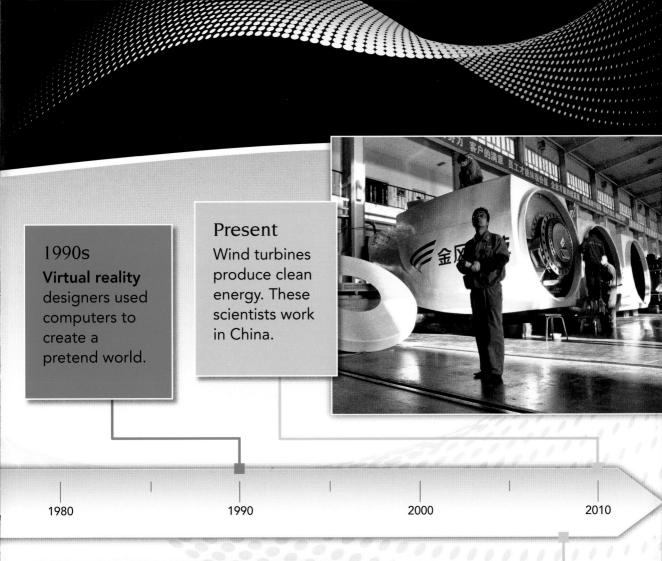

1990s
Virtual reality designers used computers to create a pretend world.

Present
Wind turbines produce clean energy. These scientists work in China.

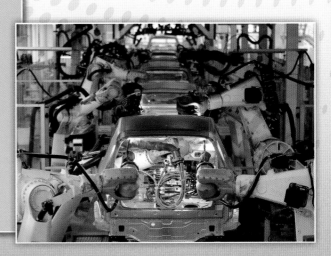

2008 ROBOTS AT WORK

In 2008 there were 1,035,900 robots working in various jobs around the world. Today, Japan uses twice as many robots as any other country in the world. Most robots work in car factories. Some are used in making chemicals, rubber products, and plastic. Other robots work in health care and medicine.

1980   1990   2000   2010

New Ways to Work

Work has changed over the years. Even ancient jobs that survive today, such as farming, cooking, and fishing, use new tools to make the work quicker and easier. How will work change in the future? Will we be doing the work ourselves, or will we create robots to do it for us?

Present MEDICAL TECHNOLOGY

This thought-controlled artificial arm works almost as well as a real arm. Medical **engineers** built the arm, surgeons attached it, and **therapists** helped the patient learn how to use it. In the future, computers and robots may help doctors find better ways to treat injuries and illnesses.

Present

Present

Data researchers study information and report the results to companies to help them plan products for the future.

Present

Robotics engineers are making smaller and smaller robots. A robotic insect like the one shown would be able to take pictures, record sounds, and check for poisons and other dangers.

Future

Passenger flights to outer space, called space tourism, might require spaceship pilots, as well as people to run space hotels and restaurants. Travel agents might find new work booking flights to the moon.

Future

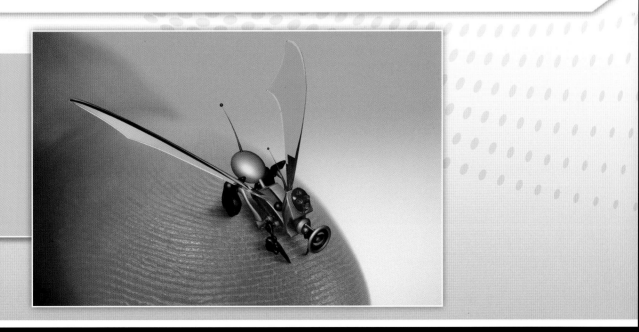

Key Dates

2.6 million years ago
Toolmakers in East Africa make digging tools from stone.

c. 4,850 BCE
Farmers in Asia begin to grow wheat and barley.

c. 3,000 BCE
Slave workers in Africa and Asia build temples, palaces, and pyramids.

Mid-1700s BCE
Hammarubi develops a code of laws, opening up jobs for court officials, judges, and lawyers.

300–200 BCE
Construction workers build temples, dig roads, and create waterways in ancient Rome.

1000s–1600s CE
In Europe, peasants work farmland owned by kings and lords. Others work as household servants and entertainers.

c. 1448
The invention of the printing press in Germany creates jobs for writers, publishers, printers, and booksellers.

1400s–1500s
Explorers travel the world.

Mid-1400s–1600s
Slave traders take captives from Africa to Europe and the Americas to work on farms and in mines.

1760s
In Britain, hundreds flock to cities to operate factory machines. Factory work spreads throughout the world.

1880s
Electrical **engineers** set up lines to bring electricity from generating plants into homes and businesses.

1900s
In the United States, the first successful airplane flight opens up jobs for pilots, as well as for airplane manufacturers and travel agents.

1940–present
Television spreads from the United States and the United Kingdom to the world, employing people in hundreds of different jobs.

1960s
The space industry employs engineers, scientists, and astronauts.

2008
More than a million robots are used worldwide to assemble cars and do other factory jobs.

Glossary

archaeologist someone who studies historic or prehistoric peoples and their cultures by looking at the things they left behind

astronomy study of outer space

caravan group traveling together carrying passengers or trade goods

chariot light, two-wheeled vehicle for one person, usually drawn by horses

civil servant person employed by the government

civilization particular society or culture at a particular period of time

colony part of the world controlled by a distant country

dynasty period of rule of a particular family

engineer someone who works with or designs engines, machines, and structures such as bridges

grain cereal grass such as wheat, corn, rye, oats, or rice

Industrial Revolution time of rapid growth of factories that began in England in the mid-1700s and spread to many other countries

lime white material found in limestone or oyster shells and used in mortar or cement

Mesopotamia part of the world we now call Iraq, as well as some parts of Syria, Turkey, and Iran

Middle East part of the world that includes southwest Asia, the Arabian Peninsula, and northeast Africa

pharaoh ruler of Egypt

philosopher person who offers views on important questions

producer person who arranges for a movie to be made by organizing all the equipment and people involved and finding the money to pay for them

programmer person who writes computer programs

slave person who is "owned" by someone else and must obey this owner

space program plans to build spacecraft and equipment, and to train people to explore space

switchboard unit containing switches and instruments necessary to complete telephone calls by hand

technician person who has special knowledge of a particular type of machine or piece of equipment

therapist person trained to help sick or wounded people to overcome physical problems

virtual reality computer-created world. You need special glasses and gloves to use virtual-reality programs.

Find Out More

Books

Coulter, Laurie, and Martha Newbigging. *Cowboys and Coffin Makers: One Hundred 19th-Century Jobs You Might Have Feared or Fancied*. Toronto: Annick, 2007.

Miller, Connie Colwell. *That's Disgusting!: Disgusting Jobs*. North Mankato, Minn.: Capstone, 2007.

O'Shei, Tim. *The World's Top Tens: The World's Most Dangerous Jobs*. North Mankato, Minn.: Capstone, 2007.

Robots: From Everyday to Out of This World. Toronto: Kids Can, 2008.

Tames, Richard. *Point of Impact: The Printing Press: A Breakthrough in Communication*. Chicago: Heinemann, 2007.

Websites

Explore careers at this U.S. government website:
www.bls.gov/k12/

Explore workplaces at this website:
www.knowitall.org/kidswork/

See images of hundreds of jobs as they were done in the past, from the 1500s to the 1900s:
http://historyofwork.iisg.nl/list_images.php

Index